THE LIFE AGREEMENT

Own The Courage To Pursue
Your Soul's Ambitions

A BOOK ABOUT SELF-FORGIVENESS,

SELF-COMMITMENT AND EMPOWERMENT

SANDRA NOEMI TORRES

STOP!

You can download the full worksheets that are within this book along with some bonuses, please go to…

www.TheLifeAgreement.com

Create an impact, leave a legacy and

change the world.

Table of Contents

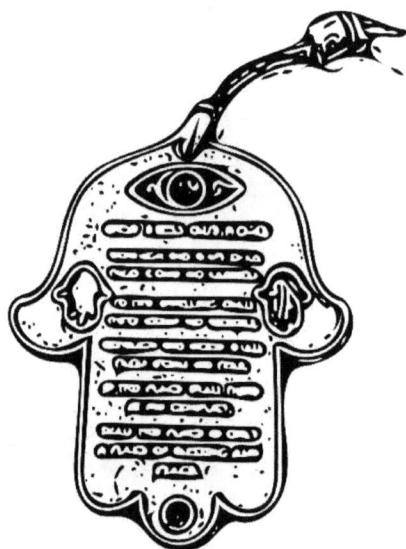

Shall these pages be a place
of blessings and of peace

ACKNOWLEDGMENTS

To my mom, I love you and I miss you every day. You will always be
remembered as the most beautiful & kindest soul who
never got to live a full life.

To my son who teaches me freedom.   May this book always remind
you of your unlimited potential to create life as you so desire it. Take
ownership and responsibility to live fruitfully and go after your
biggest dreams. This is your life, live it how you want to. Don't let
anyone ever tell you that you can't do something, including yourself.

To the collective souls who have touched my life,
May this inspire you to take action in and on your lives.
Capture every day fully, find your truth and live authentically.
Live by no-one's rules but your own.

To all the beings of the world,
You are Worthy

You Are a Gift

You Come with a Gift to Give

You are Life Force Energy

You are Evolving Consciousness

You are Gods of your Own Conscience

You are Love Manifested

You are Love Energy

You are Powerful.

You are Creator.

- The Universal Truths

PART I

ORIGIN

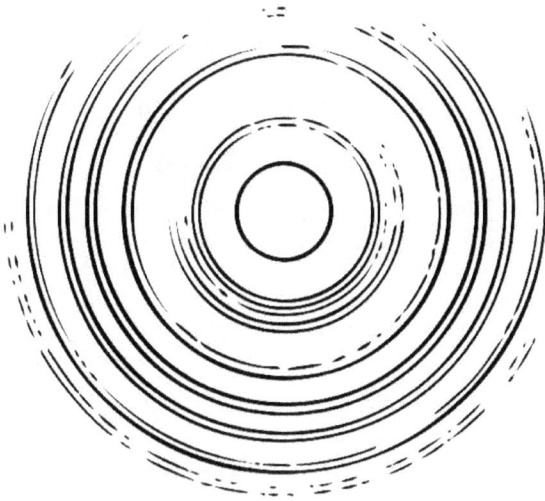

In this life you will achieve your grandest dreams

even the ones you haven't imagined yet.

Invest your time wisely.

Live for purpose & meaning.

This Life is not refundable,

Live it with intention.

CHAPTER 1

The Terms Of This Agreement

9

This book contains an agreement.

Th his agreement is between <u>You and The Universe</u> as much as it is between <u>You and Yourself</u>. This agreement addresses the subject matter of your life. And everything about it.

Who you are? How are you living? What is the significance of your life? Do you know where you're at and where you are going? What type of person do you aspire to be? Do you know what's holding you back? Who are you becoming? Yes, these are all hard questions. But knowing the answers is having a close relationship with yourself and that's the goal.

How are you treating yourself? How is your health? Do you have healthy relationships? Are you carrying around a lot of emotional baggage? What are your motives in life?

What are your professional aspirations? What business ideas do you have? How do you want to change the world?

The ultimate agreement of your life is the one of commitment of growth & evolution in your consciousness & in every aspect of your being. What do you want to do with your existence? Who do you want to become?

This is the opportunity to truly 'take hold' of what you are and what you need or want to become.

The Life Agreement gives you the key, it reminds you that you are in the drivers seat of your destiny, that you design your fate, that you are responsible for the realiziation of your dreams being manifested.

The world is changed by changed minds. And yours will begin to change the moment you embrace the fact that you have the biggest responsibility of life. And when you uncover the complex and divine responsibility, will you then be free to create and design a life that you are destined to live.

A life that makes you happy. Where you have healthy relationships with others, when you make daring career choices, where you have no drama and no true chaos. You know how to handle disagreements or atleast tame them and be reasonable and find common ground with others. You learn how to find the hope when you think thngs are bad. You are so full of self love that you can't help but love others immensely. You find your state of bliss. And learning to tap into this space' at any given time will help to heal all aspects of our lives. And suddenly success will be self defining prophesy.

This life is yours to acsend to your highest ability.

You are the one that is wholly held responsible for living out the terms of your life agreement. And you come equipped with everything you need - Your intellect. But like a muscle you must make the effort to teach your brain to evolve to it's purposed self.

This agreement was created to get you to realize the critical nature of your life, that it's not about waiting for something to change our lives but of having a responsibility to yourself and to our Source.

The facts are you have power you have not tapped into yet. May this book help you to start opening up some of those neuro doors.

This agreement is about YOUR LIFE and what YOU are about to do with it because of what you CAN do with it. It's time to move.

For the sake of us all..

There are many that understand the notion that "you only have one life to live" but there are a small few that actually live that way.

CHAPTER 2

The Immortal Promise
Of The Universe

9

"Look, if you had one shot, one opportunity to seize everything you ever wanted one moment, Would you capture it or just let it slip?"

- EMINEM

This is your moment, don't blow it.

You have waited in line to manifest yourself as a human. The odds are 400 trillion to 1 that you are even here. It's a miracle. The Universe has blessed you. Today, you have the ability to consume a thought that will change how you live out the rest of your life. You have the full authority & energy of the universe running through you – literally, And you are powerful enough to create and design your own life, your way.

The reason why most people don't achieve success are not external matters. they are all whole heartedly internal battles, a self inflicted disease whose symptoms include self doubt, fear and lack of self worth.

The Promise is that You are God's Divine. You are made from everything the Universe is made from. You are vibrating energetic love and chaos synonymously. The Sun is your sister, the Moon is your brother. God Source has blessed you with many gifts, one of them being, your own 'god-ness'. The power of your own domain. The master of your own ship. The captain of your own soul. You are in control of all of your experiences in this life.

And yet many struggle with identity. We find it easy to believe we're inadequate and difficult to truly see and accept the power of our own divinity.

So may you always remember what you know deep in your soul,

You Are Divine.

CHAPTER 3

Religious Misconceptions

9

The IDEA of God

It is an innate question in each of our minds, it's a deep desire to question the existence of God.

We were all born with the hunger. That inner burning hunger to make sense of our very existence. Why are we here? Breathing, Living, loving, hurting, crying, suffering, enjoying ? What is the purpose of Life? And how are we supposed to know if we're living it?

Many have asked themselves that very question.

What Religion holds the Truth? Who's right? Who's wrong?

Can we all be right? Can we all be wrong?

That is the question of time. It is a question that each of us will face. It isn't a coincidence. It is your inner being that was created to search for truth, to feel your source again. We were all born with the empty desire we are trying to fulfill. The connection to understanding the logic of God. And we survive as humans seeking the answers our whole lives.

The Background:
You are Already Complete.

You are energy. The spirit world is the master. And this physical world is it's servant, it is the creation of our minds, our consciousness. You are the creator and designer of your own life. You are the God of your own consciousness. Mastering our minds is the biggest struggle for mankind. Consciousness is complicated. Understanding ourselves and others and celebrating all that is good in life. Sitting and spending time meditating for your mind, this is how we can begin the journey to master ourselves.

You can decide to be in the movie of other people's life perception, or you can create and direct your own movie. You have the ability and the support from the Universe to be an A+ rated movie star of your own life.

You are an energetic field of love manifested. Damn, you are fucking awesome! And every single being you see around you, every person of every race and every religion that you can think of, they also have the same amazing energy pulsing within them. They are awesome too! They get to be alive. Life is complicated and we cannot understand why some people lose their sense of humanity and morality. But we can learn to flow with the yin and yang of life. Maintaining our own sense of peace can sometimes help others find theres.

So Who is Your God?

Religion and Spirituality is at the core of who I am as far as my favorite topics of discussions. I have and will always consider myself a life long seeker, intriqued by our humanity, seer, gnostic enthusiast and student of life.

The Pentecostal-ish times

I'm Puerto Rican, the youngest of 5 born to my mother who raised me as a single mom. I was born on the island of PR in Ponce but I grew up in central New Jersey. Although my mom and I had a daily tradition of 6am coffee, my mom and I never had any conversations about God.

She never attended church in my lifetime, that could have been the reason why her soul was so pure. hmm.. But we did go to church. My mom did send me and my sister to a Spanish Pentecostal church when I was younger. We were both the youngest, and 4 years apart. I hated getting ready on those Sunday mornings, I had to wear skirts and dresses every time and I hated it. I was very much a tomboy as a little girl.

Classes at church were divided by age groups. I was about 7 at the time and enjoyed my group. My teacher always had us read the

11

Spanish bible. I loved reading so every time she'd call for someone to read the Bible, my hand was always the first raised. And I would always get picked to read first. It became a habit after a while. She would still ask the class, but no-one else really cared to read and everyone knew I was the reader. I had an excitement for God and an anxiousness to get to know Him more. And I loved words. Everyone else was just waiting to be done with the reading so we can go play. I wanted to stay and read. I loved it. The idea that something as grand as the concept of God could be encapsulated in words was beautiful to me and I wanted to read every word that bore His name.

One Sunday while I was in the main church sanctuary with my cousins sitting in the pews by the door waiting for the van to come and take us back home, one of the other women leaders at church, turned to me, pointed her finger at me and said that 'my soul would never get to heaven, because my mother never baptized me.' I was 7 years old around this time.

While, I was never baptized at that time, I thought "how the heck would she know?" And Why would a God who I love and who's message is ultimately love abandon me for something outside of my control? I went home and told my mother that I wasn't going back, they did not know God. And I never did.

I failed at Catholic CCD

I had a best friend at the time whose family is passionate about the Catholic religion. I have attended many Saturday evening masses with her just so we can stay hanging out and playing together or during sleepovers. So my mom figured I might enjoy getting my God from there and signed me up for CCD classes at their catholic church so I could attend with my best friend at the time. I just felt ill in there. There were just too many rules of - do's and can't-do's —that seemed illogical as well and no-one could explain it to me when I asked questions. Not to mention the monotone was so boring, uninformative not to mention putting me to sleep. I lasted for 3 classes and a mass service before I quite CCD.

My Brother was Muslim

For quite a few years anyway when he was in and out of prison. Amongst some other religions he had pursued and experienced. My brother was a seeker. At the time we had moved to Monmouth County NJ. And when my brother got out of prison and moved in with us, he used to play these Muslim prayers, chants and talks. I couldn't understand them. Most of it seemed confusing to me at the time. He wouldn't care who he'd disturb, he'd play them loud in my moms small apartment. His heart always yearned for answers and to feel the "connection" fulfillment of an unwavering and literal connection to God or Allah. As one would feel "whole" again. My brother was a seeker but he became a "seer" before he died.

My Sister found Jesus

One of my sisters had found a non denominational church she was attending and was loving the version of Jesus she found there. She felt the people were genuine. The church was very accepting and not bound by strict doctrine and boring dogma. It was fun to her and the songs were beautiful, hip and inspiring and very much filled with love.

I was 20 years old when I moved to Texas with my sons father to 'start a new life with a new family in a new state with new opportunities kind of thing" when my sister handed me one of her old bibles to take with me. And that was the greatest gift of all.

I read that bible and fell in love with it. I still have that bible in my library today. It has scribbles from Jeremy when he was a toddler. Some pages have already separated from the bind, but it's written beautifully. Some pages are only held in place when the book is closed. It's got highlighter markings throughout. I have held that book and prayed with that book countless times. I have even slept with it in my hands during my most difficult times in turmoil. She changed my life the day she handed it to me, I fell in love with God's love through it. I fell in love with words and with hope. I fell in love with Psalms and humanity's thirst for hope. At that time when I didn't agree with some of the teachings, I simply tried to make sense of those parts too none the less or considered mankinds interpretation during times when the world was not as civilized.

My years surrounded by Judaism

During my 20's, I had the wonderful opportunity to work in a mostly Jewish organization. I was grateful to gain insight and be exposed to Judaism and it's fascinating spiritual construct. In fact the picture of the Hamsa at the front of this book was given to me by an old co-worker on his trip to Israel. He let me give him a prayer to put into the whaling wall and He brought me to tears when he brought me back a few gifts. I had another coworker bring me a little bag of dirt during his trip. During those times, many conversations that I had with people consisted of me asking about their beliefs, traditions and their thoughts about God and this life. I was intriqued about religions as a whole. All of them. They all fascinated me. People fascinate me. Their beliefs fascinated me, the hope of their faith fascinated me.

I wanted to dive deeper to 'why Judaism' and why were Jews consistenly saying they were the "Chosen" people? How did they come to that conclusion and certainty? I think all of us innately want to be chosen. None of us want to be left behind or valued less. Especially when our hearts know we are just struggling to be the best human we can. So what did that make the rest of us gentiles?

So then I dove deeper into the Old Testament and the origins of the Torah, and that ultimately led me to Kabbalah in my 30's. I fell in love with what I was discovering. God was not in 1 place and in 1 people.

I became fanatic about our spiritual nature and learning and consuming it all. The Universe as a grand cosmic force, the Zodiacs, Sacred geometry, Buddhism, Taoism, Hindi, The Egyptian empires, worships and hieroglyphs. Everything was starting to make sense. Everything was connected. All of these religions have the exact same thing in common. They have a vision and concept of their "IDEA of God" based on what they knew and gathered through life, their culture and upbringing.

I was consuming more and more Self Help Books, Meditating, Shamanism, Gnosticism, the Universe, Science, Psychology, Neurology. I am in love with all of it. I am in love with how diverse the Universe can express itself. How God Expresses. I am in love with being part of it. To deny it would be to deny myself, an act of self hatred. So now all things matter to me. All sentient beings, all their rights, all humans and their individual hope and journey for love from a creator. This earth and how we are treating her. She gave birth to us. It's our moral obligation to show reverence to her.

Study

You have the ability to perceive the Idea of God however one intellectually can. Keep in mind, that how you perceive the Idea of God, will impact how you approach life, how you treat others and how you walk this earth. So there is a sense of responsibility on your end to look into the truths behind the things that you believe. The evolution of your consciousness is based on your own efforts. Don't just listen to the man standing behind the pulpit. Don't believe a single word he says. Do your own digging. The answers you seek are all within you. Do not follow blindly an ideology. You must never give the power of your thought to any one practice, religion or individual. You are the sum of how you choose to think. And knowledge is everywhere. Just as this Omnipresent God Source is. And if Love is not at the core, if compassion and understanding and acceptance is not at the core, Why bother?

At the center of all beliefs of evolving consciousness is the core principle, man is the same; we want the same things – To Feel Connection.

The Journey

We will never have the same mindset. We will never all think exactly the same. And we are constantly evolving all at our own pace. But we all innately want the same basic elemental needs. Purpose for our existence, a reason for our aliveness, love from a grander parent-like/source entity that keeps guard of us in this deep dark Universe and protects us from the unknown and fragility of our mortality. We want to raise our families, experience love, love and be loved. We want to do work that is meaningful to our own hearts. We want our families to be safe.

Our paths have brought us up differently, we have each been formed by the molding of our upbringing. But ultimately we all have access to the same cosmic God power to re-energize and reconnect our lives to God. And to collectively agree that treating others with respect, decency and love is critical to our survival as a species.

The years that followed and through today were and are deeper dives down the universal possibilities and understanding of the human brain. My search is not over, I am on a beautiful journey.

All of life seeks what you seek – meaning. We all have our journey, the compilation that has developed how we have come to 'know' the concept of God.

At the root of definition: God is Love. So Be Love.

What are you doing to use your being-ness to multiply Universal love both for God and for humanity?

What I learned via my perpetual spiritual journey is to get really comfortable challenging every thing you think you know. Don't be dogmatic about a perspective. But be open to receiving God in all forms.

You are an individual
expression of God.

———

The Kingdom of God
is and has always been Within each one of us.

———

"Self worth comes from one thing
– thinking that you are worthy."

- Wayne Dyer

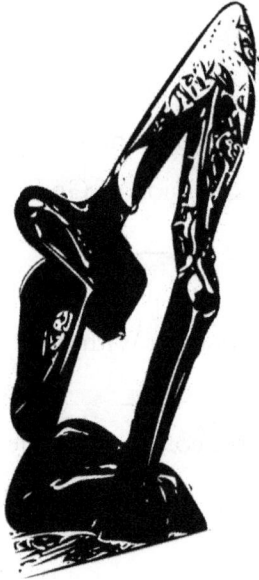

All beliefs land you in the same place.

Unanswered questions.

Everything that we truly desire from this life
is spiritual certainty.

CHAPTER 4

Time

9

Time: It's an illusion and it's also illusive.

This Life is short.

Period. That should give you a kick in the ass and for many people it doesn't. They are happy with being passengers in their own lives. But I gather if you're reading this, you may have some dreams sitting on the back burner waiting for the right time. Well, it's time.

I just celebrated 41 years on this planet. If I break that down, I have lived for 14,965 days already; 6,570 of them I was a minor and 8,395 days as an adult. If the average human lifespan is about 80 years old, that means, if I don't live longer and hopefully not shorter, I have approximately only 14,235 days left to fulfill the desires of my heart about the type of world I want to help see. We often take life for granted by taking our days for granted, we procrastinate. It's time to move our asses.

Some may think it's morbid to think about death but that's a reality of life. There's no trying to sugar coat anything here. You are either living or dying. And you need to figure out which one you are.

Not thinking about the days you have left, avoiding to come face to face with this reality will be your biggest regret. You will not live fully believing that tomorrow will come. It's an easy way to remain stagnant and believe that tomorrow will bring you another opportunity for you to chase your dreams. You are not taking advantage of your ability right now to live. And you will die next to the tombstones of your dead passions. Become very aware of your days. Wake up everyday and be grateful and then make that count.

Count Your Days

80 – your current age = _____ x 365 days =

_____ = Days left to fulfill a purpose.

You are either moving towards your dreams or away from them. There is no saving them for later. I'd like to share an excerpt that really hit home for me from a book written by Matthew Michalewics. It was given to me free in my entry bag at a trade show in NY. You never know where inspiration comes from. It's titled "Life in Half a Second" and this excerpt perfectly sums up the value of time:

"The point of it all, since the planet cooled and nature first put her hand to work, was to produce you – the finest specimen of an eternity of mutation

and adaptation, surviving the evolutionary climb of all evolutionary climbs, through miracle and chance, beating all odds, winning a trillion-to-one-wager, winning the sperm race to be born, to be you. And today, sitting comfortably, reading this book, safe, warm, fed, the beneficiary of millions of years of unimaginable suffering and billions of years of incalculable good luck, there you are, with just half a second to enjoy the result, the marvel of existing, the miracle of being. And what do you do with that half second? Something other than what you want!"

So what do you do with your time?
This Time is Yours to Manage - Life is Yours to Create.
You are the Master of your own Time:

Whether you are an entrepreneur, business owner, or professional the time you have on this earth is yours. When you work for someone you are selling your time for money. So figuring out what that is that you are willing to live for and die for is important to your happiness.

No one is responsible for your life but you. If you're one of those people that have ever blamed anyone for something that went wrong in your life, and you believe adamantly that it was their fault, this part is going to suck for you.

No one is obligated to appease to you for anything in your life. That means your success or lack there of is your responsibility.

Your failures are yours, own them. Your journey is yours and yours alone. No one owes you anything, not your kids, spouse, boyfriend, girlfriend. Your walk, your steps, you make your choices. It's no one else's fault you failed, you didn't have, you could have... should have.. would have...... It's all you at the center of your life's decisions.

You will find Freedom when you decide to Free others from the responsibility to your happiness.

Everyone else is busy creating theirs.

By the time you finish this book and worksheets, you will have gained the clarity on your purpose to create an energetic life you enjoy.

Everyone else around you is perceiving their own experiences, they are designing and learning to design their own experiences, they are busy trying to make sense of their own life. So don't demand on them, add value to them. And I'm sure you've heard.. the more of what you put out, the more of what returns.

Do things that make you happy

Matthew Michalewics', put it beautifully again when he said;

"It's the tragedies of all tragedies [...] Our lives are so cluttered doing what we "have to" that there's no room for what we "want to," even though we only have a half a second to do it. Perhaps that's why there's so much unhappiness in the world! Perhaps that's why Americans spend $57 billion on lottery tickets each year – not to win wealth, but to win freedom and finally do the things they want to. "

People don't change when they see the light. They change when they feel the heat. I have empathy for you to get yours and it doesn't happen overnight. But every day wasted is a day closer to dying not having attempted to act on your greatness.

*Remembering that you are going to die is the best way I know to **avoid the trap of thinking you have something to lose.** You are already naked. There is no reason not to follow your heart.*

- Steve Jobs

Stop acting so small.
You are the universe
in ecstatic motion.

\- RUMI

Your life is right now! It's not later! It's not in that time of retirement. It's not when the lover gets here. It's not when you've moved into the new house. It's not when you get the better job. Your life is right now. You might as well decide to start enjoying your life right now, because it's not ever going to get better than right now – until it gets better right now!

– ABRAHAM HICKS

Your Greatest Power is to Be.

To be more loving.

To be more courageous,

To be more joyous,

To be more friendly.

To be more sensitive

To be more aware

To be more forgiving

To be more tolerant

To be more humble

To be more patient

To be more helpful

To Be a Greater Human Being.

--Unknown

How can one describe the human soul
and our deep profound spiritual essence?

The God we seek
And the God that we have come to envision.

What is the purpose of our lives?
What does it all mean?
Who are we meant to be?
And what are we supposed to do with our time?

We need meaning.
We need matter.

Life is about going for it.

A 'Fuck it' mentality.

You have nothing to lose but life itself.

And that's a fact.

So don't fear the Flight.

CHAPTER 5

Evolution Of The Consciousness

9

You decide how you want to evolve in this life.

Go be you. The world needs your genius. This is the Rise of Your Consciousness. You have a dream, some of you may feel pulled to a bigger purpose but life has got you occupied with the mundane day to day.

You'll get there, you know it, you're still subtly chugging away at your passions when you're not drained from being pulled at life meeting every one else's needs and expectations. It's critical during these times to find support center if your serious. And how do you know you're serious? You really don't give a fuck about the risks involved. Your heart cannot do anything else.

You want to go after your dreams of entrepreneurship or venture but you're afraid to take the risks. You're afraid of the unknown. You're afraid to fail. You're afraid. Don't be. You win.

You Define Your Dreams

You are the designer of your life. But like it or not, ready or not sometimes our mission pulls us. We must find it. We must find our contribution to the world.

You must contribute to the bigger purpose.

This life is not just about you, you affect others in every moment in every way. So understanding your energetic role in that is critical.

You have a bigger purpose, ability and responsibility to impact this world. However small or big that may be. If you feel you are being called, it's time to rise now. It's time to unite. It's time to allow your purpose to become part of the bigger universal purpose.

The Universe Doesn't Care For Excuses – Only You Do.

There are never any excuses because the only one you will let down is yourself. No-one is responsible for the life before you but you. Every body has a story so there are not excuses given. You either want it or you don't. If you need help, ask. If you have passion, you'll find a way. Everything is possible in the world of the internet. You have to do the things necessary.

Because every body has circumstances that don't seem ideal or set them back or with a late start or with no funding. What would your life be like if you had the ability to stop making excuses for yourself and for your life?

Everybody has suffered. That is how we can relate and have empathy for each other. Now we must go and love more.

FREE Hug Challenge - Recently, I had the privilege of being involved in a group where we had an opportunity to do the "Free Hug" Challenge. The idea was to "put yourself out there" "be vulnerable" and "get rejected" face some of those fears. Over come the fear that people will reject you in life. People will say no. I discovered some very important things that day.

That when you are <u>not alone,</u> you are <u>not afraid,</u> we went out in groups, which gave each of us established bravery. We were made to not be alone and it only makes sense that we have renewed power and confidence when we attempt the things in life in partnership with another.

The people we offered hugs to seemed more scared than we were. Some people can be skeptical of a total stranger offering a hug. Some hesitated, some said no. Some just needed a push to step outside their comfort zones and then they thanked us. Some had open arms to us before we even offered. It was really cool.

The majority were <u>unbelievably grateful and receptive</u> for the kind and random act. It changed their lives that day. We changed lives that day. By a small random act of kindness offering a hug. And we changed our own lives that day. You never know the people who are waiting for your help, for your random love. And in return we all felt so blessed.

The larger majority of people had open arms. They thanked us, they appreciated it. They needed it.

When we spread more love, more hugs to the world. It has a domino effect. Those you hugged will offer some of the love you shared to another in some form. It's energy, you're energy and you can transfer positive energy this way.

The world needs your love multiplied. You got so much of it, spread some out and see what changes start to happen to your own life. You are a magnet for what you send out into the world. Send love, receive love, send kindness, receive kindness, and remember this applies to negative emotions, so don't send any, so you don't get any in return.

Humanity needs you to do what you are called to do and it's a growth process.

Growth in Your Alone Time

It's ok to go to the dark depths of the Universe. I've been there.

Go ahead we all have a safe space within us. Where you shut out the world and go into your dark room every now and then if you need to feel out your emotions or cry or lay low for a minute, but only with the knowledge that you need that time to figure out your next "what now?" We are emotional. Embrace that. You are not weak. You are beautiful. Emotions are beautiful.

Embrace Your Evolution.

In order for you to become who you need to be. Who you want to be? You need to evolve into that. And you will experience pain and hesitation.

Understand How Fear Works

Fear is going to try and stop you. Don't let it.

What would happen for you if you were able to tame & manage the fears in your life?

Take Responsibility.

What would you do if you stopped blaming your life or your circumstances for your failures and you were able to fly with the wind helping you along? You must embrace the idea of your failures, know that it is a prerequisite. But not trying, not going for things, not pushing yourself, is the ultimate failure. For it means you cannot even control yourself and then you must put yourself in a situation where you can learn the tools to do so. To evolve into who you will become, repetitively.

Find Clear Direction.

Some may experience a feeling of overwhelm and stress when they are not able to have a clear cut focus for themselves on the path they should choose. It's ok. Clarity is often found in the center of chaos.

Through self reflections, support and guidance you can often narrow down your focus into a 'particular & ultimate mission'. No-one knows which venture or plan will succeed for them, so pursue all the things that make you happy and you will find success.

Open To Experiences

Open yourself up to trying new things, to be willing and always be open. If something intrigues you, look into it.

Open To Yourself

Learn to getting more and more acquainted with yourself. Becoming Self aware. Learn how to manage your emotions, relationships and nurture yourself enough to be able to nurture another.

Love those Lives Around You

Look around you, people are going through their own crap. There is sadness everywhere. There are people carrying boulders of regrets and resentment. They are suffering. They have failed.

Many people are stuck and often live their entire lives not ever knowing or tapping into the 'power over their lives'. They simply don't know better. Like it's said, "You don't know ,what you don't know". But be open to knowing. Otherwise you will miss out.

Make yourself aware of the fact that you are not aware of everything. Most people walk around thinking they know everything that there is . The truth is that they know everything there is as it pertains to their small, short, and conditioned life. There are galaxies of thought processes you can't even fathom.

Ask the Universe for support, it listens.

Prayer Works. Source is listening.

ake sure you can handle what you're asking for?

Most people want to live rich, but they have a poor mentality. If you are dreaming of being rich I hope you are also thinking about how the possibility to even be rich could even be possible.

Also, becoming who you need, will require you to step outside your most comfortable zones. And require you to get uncomfortable so you can live your greater purposes. Most people aren't willing to get uncomfortable. Or tend to back down when the overwhelm of evolving is just to evident.

You will take your life's medicine, whether you like it or not. The evolution of your consciousness will happen in 2 ways.

2 Types of Conscious Evolution – which are you?

Voluntary - You seek growth and you are actively growing neurons as you gain new perspectives. You are the person who seeks to stretch your limbs, you seek to gain new understandings, you seek to understand the viewpoints of others. You seek to not have *an* opinion but to see the *many* opinions you have within you. You are not binary. You have evolved to be a breathing living contradiction. You are Ying and Yang in one. You have fluidity in your opinions and in your thoughts.

Involuntary – You will grow regardless, you will learn regardless. But you will not have initiated this growth. You are a spectator of life. You will learn what is presented. But you are not a seeker of ultimate truths. You are binary. The world is black and white. It's the left and the right. You don't question rules. You have solidified opinions based on what you are told to think.

The 3 Ways to See the World.

There are 3 point of sights that affect how you consume and perceive your world, your purpose, power and life here on earth.

The first of these is your obvious Eye, I'm referring to your eyeball that sits on your face that's reading this right now. It's your natural ability to see colors, objects and material matters. Don't need any explaining there. But do you always trust what your eyes see? And most importantly are you aware of the 99% you don't see.

You can see a forest of trees but you can literally 'see' a forest of trees with your heart as well. That is the second type of sight. Your ability to see through something and see meaning and purpose within it. I see beauty in nature. The greenery of life is profound to me. I see Mother Earth and her Divine Feminine beauty. I see God in everything - Your Heart vision. You see with points of view such as love, admiration, compassion and empathy.

And lastly there is the Point of Understanding. And it entails the use of the 3rd eye. Those "aha' moments' You finally can 'see' what someone is talking about or you have figured something out, or you can see it in a new light or new perspective. Understanding is very vast and fluid. The pineal gland also referred to as "The third eye refers to the gate that leads to inner realms and spaces of higher consciousness" It is where you can feel your most spiritually connected to all life and time.

"I wish for you a life of wealth, health
and happiness; a life in which you give to
yourself the gift of patience, the virtue of reason,
the value of knowledge, and the influence
of faith in your own ability to dream about and

TO ACHIEVE
WORTHY REWARDS."

◆

*"The Price of Greatness
is Responsibility."*

- GEORGE W BUSH

◆

*"And in the end it's not the years in your life that
matters, it's the life in your years."*

– ABRAHAM LINCOLN

PART 2

CLARITY & DECISIONS

DECIDE.

CHAPTER 6

Clarity To Dream

9

"A man's reach should exceed his grasp,
or else what's heaven for?"

- UNKNOWN

The Universe is pulling you to do something greater.

Go after your crazy idea, Follow your own heart, Why the heck not?

In this chapter, it's about helping you to become clear on **what** you want, even if you're not even clear at all on what you want. It's about how to do something you want today and tomorrow that is growing you, that is challenging you. Since, steps are taking one after the other, we become only to the depths of what we feel we are capable of becoming, and then only what we take Action to become.

It's about Dreams, and dreaming big, nothing is out of your reach.

Whatever dream you are holding within your heart to fulfill, you have the ability within you to manifest it outward.

> **You are absolutely responsible and obligated to pursue the dreams in your heart.**

No excuses - You cannot put blame on anyone or anything.

You must work hard to manifest them. Who we become is 1 portion of our aspirations and 99% of our actions. Dreaming is beautiful, but Daring to fulfill them is bold. It is the exception sadly as most people never dareto dream, never dare to believe that it's even possible.

Practicing the "law of attraction" often puts us into a euphoric state of hope and joy. But what's the point if you don't take bold action in pursuing them?

If you're not 100% clear and committed to accomplish what you want to accomplish you are not going to cut it in manifesting your dreams. No one can take that journey to fulfill your dreams for you, no one is going to knock on your door and hand deliver them to you. So what are you going to do today to get yourself closer to accomplishing your dreams?

The Man on the Curb – A Story about Inspiration

I saw a man sitting on a curb.

He was walking crossing with his camo' shorts, white T, and white Nike hi-tops w/ red swoosh. He walked with a swag, looking around, taking in the business of that intersection, inhaling life it seemed. He was walking briskly like he had somewhere he needed to go. Then suddenly, he stopped. He took a backstrap of his back and was looking for a seat, so he grabbed a piece of the curb. He took out a pad and something to write or draw with, at first I didn't know what he was doing. Then he became emerged. He was so emerged into whatever he was doing, as if he was relieving himself of something beautiful inside him. Something that needed to be expressed, even if he was the only one to see it. And I almost sensed the peace he got during this exhilaration. I thought it was beautiful. We all get inspired by life. We all have our own form of self expression, what is for us, isn't for others. Just as what is for others, isn't always for us. We have our own way, but non the less, there is a way. The human must self express.

His book-bag lay opened next to him. I could see a box of opened colored pencils, and some other pads. It was inevitably a very comfortable form of expression for him. He was inspired and I was inspired by him.

When we dream, we must have this same type of passion and inspiration.

It is truly up to you to pursue all that is within your heart.

What's most important to you when you dream? What do you dream about? What strikes a chord in your heart? What stops you in your tracks and gets you entranced with passion? What is your form of self expression and what are those thoughts that fascinate you most about your life or humanity and your role in it?

When thinking about your dreams, these are some good questions to ponder.

What do you stand for in life? What are your values, morals?

_____

_____

_____

_____

What is your belief about the world around you?

_____

_____

_____

_____

Be Free to Dream and make sure you are creating experiences along the way.

Creating Experiences

You get to decide what things make you happy and fulfill you most and you should go do those things. I believe the experience of success in life is uniquely defined by our happiness and that's defined by what's most important to each person. Go do what makes you happy. Life is pointless if you're not enjoying the journey your way. But be mindful and true to yourself that you are doing things that elevate your consciousness, utilize the beauty of your body and be creative in how you choose to live and give to life.

What are your Big & Little Dreams?

_____

_____

_____

_____

What do you dream about? What do you want to accomplish? What calls to you?

How do you or will you paint the picture of your life?

How do you want to leave the world?

How will you be remembered?

What fascinates you?

_____

_____

_____

_____

_____

_____

_____

Nothing is beyond the realm of possibility. There are no limitations except the limits of your own imagination.

– DOLORES CANNON

Don't sit on the sidelines waiting for things to change. Take charge and make your dreams come true.

- JOHN ASSARAF

The 4 Areas of Goals

Your dreams and goals should be separated by categories. It's important to separate them because it allows you to grow in all areas simultaneously, making it easy for real change when you are now creating habits that affect multiple areas of your life.

Clarity of Goals Worksheets:

Setting Specific Goals to gain clarity and focus

Ideas to explore include and are not limited to the below

1) Your Mind

Meditation, Yoga, Martial arts, Fitness, Mantras, Conscious Eating, Go Plant Based, Travel more, be in nature. Do things that enhance your mental state of being.

2) Your Body

Yoga, Boxing, Sports, Fitness Program

What are the dreams/goals that you have for your health? Your body? Nutrition? Be mindful.

"You are what you eat, so don't be fast or cheap."

3) Your Relationships

Family, Loved ones, Friends, Network. Maintaining openness and connection to others. What are the dreams that you have for **your**

relationships? What kinds of relationships do you want to have? And are you taking responsibility in the matter?

4) Your Business / Career

Reading, learning more about your own business or professional industry, attending industry conferences and events, networking, Grow your business. Social missions, impacts. What are the dreams and aspirations for **your 'business'?** And make sure it makes you happy.

These 4 major areas of your life need thoughtful attention. When you write out your goals. Write out goals in every category here.

Your health, your mindset , your relationships and your business so here you can start putting pen to paper and write them out. What are your dreams for each of these areas in your life?

1. What are the dreams/goals that you have for your Mental state of being?

_____

_____

_____

_____

2. What are your dreams for your Body?

_____

_____

_____

_____

3. What are the dreams that you have for your Business?

_____

_____

_____

_____

4. What are the dreams that you have for your Relationships?

_____

_____

_____

_____

Allow yourself the freedom to think big. What aspirations dwell within the centers of your heart?

It's important to have clarity when it comes to our goals. To know what you're aiming for. Next we'll discuss your Why? And then some Hows?

Note: You can download the full worksheet to this and others at www.TheLifeAgreement.com

It always seems impossible until it's done.

– NELSON MANDELA

CHAPTER 7

Purpose

9

Purpose: **T**he reason for which something exists or is done, made.

Purpose is your reason for doing anything, your **WHY**.

We are much better at knowing what we want to do than knowing why we want to do it. But knowing Why something important to you will higher the odds of being successful at it. Why does 'it' matter to you?

This is a very hard question for some to answer because it's asking you to have words that clearly pinpoint some of the 'god-ness, emotional, meaning within you.

Wherever it comes from. Whatever reason you have. It's yours. And it is your gift. And being able to express it will increase your odds of success.

Purpose can be difficult for some to identify. This journey can take years of self discovery and self awareness and courage. Because admitting to yourself what your purpose is makes you responsible to take action to do it. And most of those actions will require you to step outside your comfort zone. It may bring fear and hesitancy. It's designed to for you to use your greatness. And you will have to overcome battles of self limiting beliefs.

The journey of living with purpose is not for the weak hearted. It's for the brave. And everyone's bravery lies within, you just have to want to discover it. Discover your Why.

Be open for purpose to flow to you. You do not need to know it or have it solidified yet. But it is primarily thought of as a 'higher purpose' meaning something bigger than you, because purpose by very nature impacts lives outside of you. It's the ability to use your gifts to help the collective.

Because you are both created and created to create. There are **2 types of purpose** we're talking about. The first one – The Universe assigns you. A higher calling, a bigger purpose, people you need to help, people whose paths you will cross for a day, a moment or a lifetime, it's something you innately be called to do. Identifying it will give you confidence in the meaning of your life.

The Purpose of Joy & Creating a Life Full of Experiences:

It's not always all work. One of the most important things in my life that I have come to truly understand is the importance of experiences over things. I want to travel the countryside. I want to visit all the parks of this great country. I want to see every ocean view. I want to see my son enjoy all of those things too. And I feel that is part of my soul's deep purpose because it calls to me.

You Better Be Happy, Cause Otherwise there's no point.

Happiness is defined by your own individual acceptance of what is and your own individual gratitude and appreciation for your life and your ability to purposely impress upon it.

What makes one person happy will not make another. Find what makes you happy. Your version of happiness is unique to you. You don't have to conform to any societal structure. You don't have to conform. Period. Live by your rules, so long as you always take ownership and responsibility for it all.

If you want to live in a van and travel the country or speak at large stages and inspire the world. Or if you want to have a home on the water or the city. You can be successful living life and experience your existence your unique and perfect way. Whatever you decide to do, define your success by your level of joy in helping others.

Universal purpose comes in all forms, sometimes you will never know it's going on. It can even be in the most mundane but sometimes coincidental of life. Maybe you couldn't leave your house on time and forgot something and had to rush back home. That delay in timeline impacts the crossroads of souls and people you meet that day.

Your life will bring you towards it without much effort from your end other than a cause. You may even draw it to you and it may even occur in those shocking moments of "life's comes around full circle" feeling, something you encountered years ago some how shows up again in your life.

And then there is the purpose you assign yourself. Your true WHY. The things you intend to do and why does it matter to you.

Where do you want to help and why? Where do you want to pour effort into? What subjects interest you the most? Advocacy, community outreach, politics, family and children, illness, a cause?Your purpose is usually the sum of experiences in your life. Whether good or bad, your WHY is because you have a part of you that feels empathetic or compassionate about something,

It will add fuel to your life. It will give you reason to get excited about getting up and living this life. Because you are expressing love. When you find your purpose, you will find your way of expressing love out to the universe.

You have been given the task to uncover your first purpose and create your second.

It can be difficult to ponder on your purpose. For some, it's easy. Their gifts exude from them and you know instantly what they are able to bring to humanity. But for others, especially today, it can be very difficult and stressful. We all just want to know without thinking too much about it what the heck we are supposed to do so we can be confident and do it.

It is a gift for you to discover your purpose. It's your life's puzzle. Have fun with it. It can be whatever you desire it to be. Because the odds are that your heart and gut will lead you there.

Let Love Lead

One of your basic simple purposes in this life is to love others and extend compassion. When you are shown love for what you are you become your best self. The same goes for others, when you show others unconditional love, you allow them the freedom to be their best self.

Write Out Your 2 Types of Purpose

1) The Universe assigns you. A higher calling includes being the mother to your children, or not having children, a calling to be an artist, or being there to help a stranger.. because it affects the timeline of life.

2) Set an Intention or goal for oneself. The purpose you assign yourself (eg. Help the homeless, empower women, build a nonprofit) and why.

Sometimes these will be the same but throughout your entire life you will have countless defining moments that are part of your purpose, some of them part of a grander reason and some because you felt like doing it.

Mini-Worksheet

So what do you feel called to do? _____

What people do you feel called to help? _____

What are injustices that you feel you want to help correct? _____

What is your current work and do you feel it is aligned with the people that you want to help? Or can it open up opportunities for you to get yourself to a position where you can impact the lives of those that you feel called to helping?

If this was the last day of your life? What would you have wanted to have accomplished?

1) What purpose do you feel called from the Universe?

_____

_____

And Why?

_____

_____

2) What purpose do you give yourself?

_____

_____

And Why?

_____

_____

CHAPTER 8

Developing Your Mission

9

Mission is Servitude in Motion.

Mission is your How.

What is your soul's mission? Your big goals? What task have you here to accomplish? What issues are you willing to tackle? Or what truths are you here to share? Whatever you choose, your mission involves your service to humanity. What have you been called to do, affect, impact or inspire humanity?

*A Mission is an important assignment **carried out**.*

The mission's truth is resolute, the execution of your purpose. The way to get there and the time it will take can happen a myriad of ways. Depending on your choices. Your mission will involve the actual tasks involved in creating your dreams and fulfilling your purpose.

"Create the things you wish existed."
"If you can't stop thinking about it,
don't stop working for it."

Writing your personal mission is fun. This is where you paint the canvas of your life and allow yourself to dream wild and big.. and for the right reasons.

For the complete worksheet go online.

The Personal Misssion (Internal)

_____

_____

The Goals and Objectives of Your Life Plan (Internal goals)

_____

_____

_____

The Professional and Purpose Filled Life Goals (External goals)

_____

_____

_____

THE BREAKDOWN

1) What are the top goals for your (1) Business/Career this year?

_____

_____

_____

(b) What are things you can do to get there?

_____

_____

2) What are the top goals for your (2)Health this year?

_____

_____

(b) What are things you can do to get there?

_____

_____

3) What are the top goals to improve (3) MIND & Mental State of Being this year?

_____

_____

(b) What are things you can do to get there?

_____

_____

4) What are the top goals for your (4) Relationships this year?

_____

_____

(b) What are things you can do get there?

_____

_____

What you will accomplish in the next 90 Day.

Now based on what you wrote above you will chomp that down and set goals for just the next 90 Days and then 30 days, and then each week. Dividing your big goals up into small manageable chunks.

Fulfilling Your Life Mission

Setting & writing down your LIFE GOALS is important. Setting Annual goals are great. But chomping them down to absorbable pieces is critical to their manifestation and to your sense of accomplishment.

Clarify Your 90 Day Goals for all the areas that matter.

_____

_____

GOALS	30 Days	60 Days	90 Days
Business / Career			
Body			
Mind			
Relationships			

Complete worksheet available at TheLifeAgreement.com

| Business/ Career Goals |

What are your business/career goals for the next **90 days?**

_____

_____

What are your business/career goals for the next **30 days so that you can meet your 90 day goal?**

_____

_____

| Body | Health (Food & Fitness) |

What are your health goals for the next **90 days?**

_____

_____

What are your health goals for the next **30 days so that you can meet your 90 day goal?**

_____

_____

_____

| Mind (Mental, Spiritual, Emotional) |

What are your mind goals for the next **90 days?**

_____

_____

_____

What are your mind goals for the next **30 days so that you can meet your 90 day goal?**

_____

_____

_____

Relationships (Personal & Professional)

What are your relationship goals for the next **90 days?**

_____

_____

_____

What are your relationship goals for the next **30 days so that you can meet your 90 day goal?**

_____

_____

_____

Now that you have a plan for the next 90 days. Let's work on the weekly and daily habits that will help you achieve the first goal you have set for your first 30 days.

What do you need to accomplish this week to reach your 30 day goal.

GOAL AREAS	THIS WEEK'S GOALS
Business	
Body	
Mind	
Relationships	

What are your business goals for the next & **each week?**

What are your body & health goals for the next & **each week?**

What are your mental health goals for the next & **each week?**

What are your relationship goals for the next & **each week?**

WHAT WILL YOU DO TODAY?
<u>**What are the daily activities you need to commit to?**</u>

Preparing for the boulders.

In life, it's important to have a develop the plan of how you will achieve these goals. And it's also important to prepare for obstacles that could stop you or prevent you from moving forward with your mission of fulfilling your purpose and achieving your goals and dreams.

1. What's the biggest challenge you are experiencing right now?

_____

_____

What are ways to overcome them?

_____

_____

2. What are possible Obstacles that could arise?

_____

_____

How can I prepare for and have a plan in place to overcome some of those obstacles? What are things I can do?

_____

_____

Know Where To Get Support:

Identify what your good at and what you're not. This will help you build confidence and tell you where you need to seek out support.

Strengths

_____

_____

Weaknesses

_____

_____

Extra Bonus: Social worksheets

I also included 2 additional partial worksheets that can help on narrowing your social mission(s) in this life. And you can download the full worksheets online at TheLifeAgreement.com. Remember, serving humanity doesn't have to be on a large scale, it can be as simple as making sure your neighbor has a warm meal everyday. But I gather most of you reading this have a heart to do those and bigger things in life. In any case, these questions will help you look inside yourself to pull out matters that deeply impact your heart. It can be 1 or many. The destiny within your life is your unique and perfect journey bound by no rules. So you decide that. You decide what your mission will be.

Advocacy & Servitude:

"Our lives begin to end the day we become silent about things that matter." **MLK**

1) What are the injustices you feel exist?

2) What do you feel is broken with our political system?

3) Where do you feel the change needs to happen first?

4) Why does this issue bother you?

5) Do you feel you can do anything about this issue?

6) How do you feel you can help this issue?

7) What do you wish would change?

Let's work on Being that.

"Never doubt that a small group of thoughtful committed citizens can change the world; Indeed, it is the only thing that ever has."

– MARGARET MEAD.

General Social Impact:

1) How do I want to serve humanity / my tribe?

2) What do I want my tribe to gain?

3) WHY do I want to serve others?

4) How can I help right now?

5) How do I see myself helping in the future?

6) How can they fully gain the benefits?

7) How will I know if they are better?

Focus on what you need to do >>>

Nothing will work unless you do.
- Maya Angelou

You won't get distracted by comparison, if we're captivated by purpose.
- Bob Hoff

Let yourself be silently drawn
by the stronger pull
of what you really love.
- Rumi

"This is the world we live in,
And these are the hands we're given.
Use them and let's start trying,
To make this a place worth living in."
- Genesis

Small daily improvements
are the key
to staggering
long-term results.

"The secret to change is
to focus all of your energy
not on fighting the old,
but on building the new."
Socrates

We become only

to the depths of

what we feel we are capable

of becoming.

And only

what we take action

in becoming.

The Secret of getting ahead

is getting started.

The Secret of getting started is breaking
your complex,

overwhelming tasks

into small,

manageable tasks,

and then starting

on the first

one.

Mark Twain

If you care enough about the result,
you will almost always attain it.

- William James

"Don't focus on what you can't do...

Focus on what you can.

Can't will die from lack of
attention!"

CHAPTER 9

AUDACITY & COMMITMENT

9

Audacity is Boldness and Belief
in Both Your Self
and The Universe that Supports You..

You are responsible for your life's evolution. Whatever you feel you want to do and even what you want to improve upon yourself. Do it. Take action towards creating your self. Be Bold and Unapologetic about it.

What are the Habits you need to add & release in order to make the possibility of reaching these goals possible? So you know what your goals are, you have visualized those. What does exceeding those goals look like? Can you visualize that and write that down?

Create your minimum Baseline Goal and then create your Breakthrough and Badass level goals. You can download the full and more in depth worksheet at TheLifeAgreement.com. There is so much power in the process of writing and visually seeing your goals and ambitions on paper. This work guide will help you tremendously in that process.

90 Day Goals

	Baseline Goal	Breakthrough	Badass
BUSINESS			
BODY			
MIND			
RELATIONSHIPS			

"Vision is not enough. It must be combined with venture. It is not enough to stare up the steps, we must step up the steps."

- Vaclau Havel.

Go after your dream no matter how unattainable
others think it is.

– John Assaraf

"You don't have to be great to start,
but you have to start, to be great.

- Zig Ziglar

Every risk is worth taking as long as it's for a good cause, and contributes to a good
life"

– Richard Branson

"No one ever made a difference
by being like everyone else."

- P.T. Barnum

Don't live with regret.

"No one can tell your story so tell it yourself.
No one can write your story so write it yourself"

"Remember who you are. Without the number on the scale, your report
card or your bank account. Without the amount of friends you have, or
the expensive things you own. Know who you are; your raw, true self. "

"Don't wait for miracles,
your whole life is a miracle."

– ALBERT EINSTEIN

Who we become is
1 portion of our aspirations
and 99% of our actions.

"All the breaks you need in life wait within your imagination.
Imagination is the workshop of your mind, capable of turning mind
energy into accomplishment and wealth." Napoleon Hill
"Take Risks:

If you win, you'll be happy:
If you lose, you'll be wise."

Regret is misery. Go get it.

CHAPTER 10

A Habit To Habit

9

Everybody has dreams.
Go out and do it.

So we have a vision of who we are and what it is we'd like to do. Now it's about ways to kick our own ass because S.H.I.T. doesn't happen on it's own.

Who we become in life is a portion of our ambitions and 100% of our actions in its pursuit.

John Assaraf always says "Knowledge is not power, applied knowledge is power." So let's apply some knowledge that's going to give power.

HABITS

As powerful as goals are they will never be enough to get you to take action. But habits by their very nature are ongoing. They are items that never get crossed off the list. They become part of your being. You tend to do them habitually. At least until you replace that habit or release it all together if it no longer serves you or is bad for you.

But goals are needed in order to create good habits.

Because it's important to formulate habits that are centered around your goals. Habits are the stepping stones needed to get you to achieve milestones along your climb. What we repeatedly do becomes us. If we repeatedly do habits that keep us in low energy, lazy or distract us from the bigger purpose, maybe they need to be looked at. If they are habits you feel you know you want to do, then incorporate them into your day and stop making excuses.

Habits are behaviors that happen consistently over time.

The basis is extremely simple, but the concept changes shit in your brain on a cellular level.

Since humans hate change, the best scenario found is the Start 1 Stop 1 . Select only 1 habit you will start doing and pick 1 bad habit you will release. But if you can do several at once, go for it.

The best way to success is a clear definitive and flexible plan of attack. But the point here is to have a plan.

Choose an important goal over the next 90 days and create habits, daily habits that inch you towards that goal.

"Changing habitual behavior is a process. Be patient and be compassionate with yourself. Each of us creates our own journey of releasing bad habits and adopting good habits through conscious choice. Embrace those choices; embrace the changes. They are the catalysts that will improve your life."

– RITA SCHIANO

"If you spend to much time thinking about a thing, you'll never get it done. Make at least one definite move daily toward your goal."

– BRUCE LEE

Mini Habit Worksheet

What are habits that you feel you need to release?

_____

What are habits you feel you need to add into your life?

_____

What is your big **WHY** for wanting to commit to changing bad habits into good?

_____

"Live for the iron and the fresh air. Punish your body to protect your soul. Only acts undertaken with commitment have meaning. Only your best effort matters. Life is a meritocracy, with death as the auditor. Inconsistency, incompetence and lies are all cut short by that final word. Death will change you if you can't change yourself."

- MARK TWIGHT.

You have to do the things you don't want to do so you can be who you need to be. The magic in the formula to understanding what success really is, is the understanding that it's finally discovering you are the master creator of your own world.
Take Action.

"A River cuts through a rock
not because of its power
but it's persistence."

◆

The Secret of getting ahead
is getting started.
The Secret of getting started is
breaking your complex,
overwhelming tasks
into small,
manageable tasks,
and then starting
on the first
one.

MARK TWAIN

PART 3

SOUL WORK

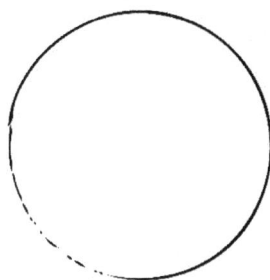

The World is Suffering, You are Not Alone

Nothing is easy, if achieving success and doing all these things were easy, more people would achieve it. The fact of the matter is the world is suffering. We all have battles. We all have to fight our own negative thoughts & demons. This is were you can forgive yourself and learn to love all that is.

CHAPTER 11

Pillar Of Courage

9

Courage is the price that life exacts for granting peace.

– AMELIA EARHART

I left Plano, Texas on a shuttle bus to Dallas International with a 2 year old boy, no drivers license, no college education, no job and $30 in my pockets.

This was my first leap of courage when I was a 20 year old, a new mom and separating from my sons father.

Moving back home to my mom's 1 bedroom apartment in New Jersey, where my sister and my brother were currently also staying. Too often many people stay stuck in situations that are not good for them because they don't have the courage to move forward. Leaving my sons father and deciding I wasn't going to limit my life was not a hard decision. My value is in my sanity and I wasn't going to be a prisoner of a life I didn't love. I wasn't happy, I knew I couldn't be the mother I needed to be for my son and I could not be the right woman for my son's father. I was not willing to stay.

Was it scary making this decision on my own? Yes. But what scared me more was being trapped in sadness.

Courage comes from the attitude of 'not willing' to stay stuck. 'Not willing' to not move forward.

I'm the youngest of 5, courage is in my DNA. I looked up to everyone and wanted to care for them because I loved them. So I was bold. Bold in my thoughts and bold in my audacity to believing we did not have to be slaves to a system that told and taught us how to live.

I was an entrepreneur at a very young age. I still have visions of the business I owned when I was 6. I have a feeling it will come full circle again in my life. We will see what I make of it. But none-the-less. There's a sense of audacity. A claim. Claim what is yours. And what is yours is everything you are willing to create and work for. Everything.

BOLD Courage

To have it don't psyche yourself out.

Take advantage of all of the opportunities life presents you that are aligned with your mission. The scarier ones, the better. Those are the steps you will need to climb to achieve and become the man or woman you aspire to.

What scares you?

Whether you are a professional and putting yourself out there scares you, fear of public speaking or if you're in sales often the fear of rejection can overcome people.

What are your beliefs about what scares you?

Many of you will probably not know how to answer this question, because you fears are typically unfound. Meaning there usually is no really logical reason or detrimental result that will occur when you decide to push through a fear and do it.

Fear of public humiliation is no reason to not pursue the calling on yourself to speak up and use your voice.

What are you biggest fears when it comes to overcoming your fears?

What scares you when it comes to your professional aspirations?_____

Why? _____

Is what you fear the worst thing in the world? _____

Too many people are out there doubting their capabilities.

We worry that we really don't have what it takes to become who we need to be. We lose our bravery. We lose faith in our ability to push through when we get punched in the gut.

But then it's up to us to kick our own ass.

How can we find the courage to overcome the past?

Carrying the burden of your painful pasts is significant. And it's hard to let go. Sometimes our stories are too sad, but sometimes we depend on them to save us. We start to use them as excuses for not moving the needle along.

When the world treats us bad, we find strength in what we have already endured in our lives. Courage is in your ability to think, 'you have been through these hard things, you can take on the next thing that comes along.'

Feeling weak is often how many people feel strong.

Innate Boldness

Many of you have this. It's the guts. It's the audacity.

"We suffer more in imagination than in reality."
Seneca

You are responsible for your life's evolution. Whatever you feel you want to improve upon, do it. Take action towards creating your self.

Be Bold and Unapologetic about it.

"Everything you want
is on the other side of fear."

– JACK CANFIELD

*"He who is not courageous enough to take risks
will accomplish nothing in life."*

- MUHAMMED ALI

*"In any given moment we have two options: to step forward into growth or to step
back into safety.*

– ABRAHAM MASLOW

*"If you can't fly then run, If you can't run then walk,
If you can't walk then crawl, but whatever you do
you have to keep moving forward."*

- MLK JR

*"Success is not final, failure is not fatal: it is the
courage to continue that counts"*

– WINSTON CHURCHILL

*"Nothing happens to any man
which he is not formed by nature to bear"*

– MARCUS AURELIUS

"We are realists – realists who expect

a miracle every day."

- UNKNOWN

"At the end of the day,
on the wings of your thoughts,
go beyond the cares and troubles
of the world.
Remove your mind from everything
and everyone,
and become blissfully detached,
like a star."

- BRAHMAKAMRAIS

it easier to live in the world they've been given than to explore the power they have to change it. Impossible is not a fact. It's an opinion. Impossible is not a declaration. It's a dare. Impossible is potential. Impossible is temporary. Impossible is nothing."

MUHAMMED ALI

CHAPTER 12

Suferring

9

"The root of suffering is attachment."

BUDDHA

Let's face it, doing all these things and accomplishing our dreams isn't always easy. There are many things that hold many people back. Many of it internal. There is a price to the luxury of your humanity. There are also support systems in place. The Pillars are made up of everything that you will need to support you on your journey. They are in no particular order. They are all vital.

There are a few moments or memories that have caused me suffering, these are the ones that bring me the most emotions.

Can a Caged Bird Fly Free?

When I was 21 years old and new mom, I lost my spiritual seeking, drug addicted brother to a heroin overdose. He was found dead in a motel room where he lived. 8 months later my mother 53 years old at the time was diagnosed with advanced alzheimerz.

My mother finally passed in 2011 at the age of 65. And throughout all those years I was trapped in a prison of regret I had built myself. It included massive resentment and unfathomable sadness.

Regret

I regretted how I treated her those last few years as a careless & rebellious teen. We didn't have cell phones back then. So sometimes I'd sleep out and never call home. My mom was worried and I didn't care. I let her suffer and I hated myself for that for a long time.

My mother's diagnosis with alzheimerz was the scariest moment of my life. My faith in life was shaken.

The beginning of the end.

It was June of 1999, about 8 months after my brothers death. I was at work when I received a call from my sister, she said my mom's job called her and there was an incident with my mom and her work, she was a bus driver for the city. She said to me "Sandra, we need to take mom to a doctor tomorrow and I need you to take the day off and come with me."

You see, my mother had been forgetting stuff. The typical stuff, keys, minor thoughts process, things that happen to you at 53 years old, but this was different. Something was really wrong this time. She was making too many mistakes.

I was scared, we were all scared, my life and the vision I had for my future would forever be changed.

I remember this day so clearly, it haunts me. I still remember how cold that doctors office felt, the room they sent us to, the all white walls. My mom didn't want to sit on the doctors bed so we all were just standing there holding hands when the doctor walked in. I remember the uneasy feeling all of us were having at what the doctor would say. Or what he needed to do to run tests. Can we fix what's going on? We needed answers?

The doctor comes in and asks my mom the first question, "What is your name?" My mom sweetly smiled and said it, "Anaida." And then the second question "What year is it?" and my mother with a nervous smile, hesitated a bit and responded with "1995."

We all knew instantly, this was the beginning of the end.

My mother always had a smile, even when she was scared inside. She never let anyone see her sweat. Those shy, timid smiles, those "I hope I don't say the wrong thing, smile" I still remember them. She had a glow of innocence when she smiled. She lit up the room with her love.

And I guess that's where my prison sentence began.

How can God allow something so cruel to happen to someone so beautiful? Alzheimerz is a cruel disease. My moms entire demeanor had changed since my brothers death. She became submissive, her daughters were now in complete charge of her life. So she went to go live with my oldest sister in Union County and I was on a mission to afford my first apartment for my son and I.

My Son and I had

My son was just 3 years old during this time. he had lost his favorite & only uncle and his loving grandmother. It was a sink or swim mentality now and I had no-one to really depend on. Sure I had my sisters but they all had their own home and families. I was an adult, a single young mom and I had to get an apartment and build a life for me and my son. I knew no-one was obligated to help me.

My internal battles:

How can I have lost her? I still ask this to myself sometimes. I have not even begun to tell her how sorry I was for being a rebellious teen. For not calling, for making her worry, for probably making her feel like I didn't love her with those actions. I needed her. I need to tell her I sorry I was.

My son needed her. Her love, her hugs, her passion for others. She was the example of love. He was everything to her. She loved him so much.

My son was robbed. I was robbed. For many years I was simply utterly sad. She didn't deserve to go out like this. It just wasn't fair. She was alive and breathing but could no longer recognize her children or her self. That was heartbreaking to be an observer of. I was mad at God. I questioned everything I thought I knew.

God doesn't favor your faith over another

I have learned there is no right religion, God will not favor you over someone else who does not believe in "him". God is not Christian, He is not Jew or Muslim or Buddhist Or Taoist or Non denominational or Catholic or Atheist... God is.. He is all of the above, every light and every dark.

When someone envisions God in their image, they are limited. God is not a man that makes decisions. God is the soul of the universe and all its cosmic intelligence, the good and the bad... and that includes us. We are god. We are each pieces of his grandness.. of his robe. And we play a key role in the direction of our own lives.

I needed to make logic of all this. I needed to find spiritual purpose in the fact that I lost a woman who was kind and loving, accepting and forgiving.. and whom I have never ever seen angry.

My fear was that God was not in control because if He were, something this evil wouldn't have happened. Something this terrible. Having a shell of a body with no human mind behind it?

What kind of spiritual existence is that? My fear was that we were not in control either, life was going to treat us as nasty as it wanted.

Buddha was right "All life is suffering"

And that was my biggest fear of all for a while. Because it took away the hope for love being at the center of all and for my life to have any form of meaning or purpose. I was sad. And I've been mourning my mother since the diagnosis.

The Smile that hides your sorrows

Sure, I had accomplished professional successes during this time. I did what most humans like me have to do, smile and keep it moving. Life must go on, bills need to get paid. And then one day, your existence will be a thing of the past. And who you were are but memories in the lives of those closest to you.

Life began to take a new meaning, a bigger purpose. To leave a legacy, to leave my kid with something, to matter to people. I realized then, trials are mandatory for everyone, suffering is a choice.

Not Giving control over to you sorrows.

To give the events in my life more power than my ability to overcome them seemed wrong to me. The strength we possess as humans can move mountains and I wasn't going to allow it to destroy me from the inside. But deep inside it was slowly eating at me.

I carried my share of baggage and kept faith in the love that the universe has for me, that God has for me. I held onto the fact that I had immense love inside me that needed an outlet. I could no longer hug my mother, but I wanted to hug the world.

I was suffering and I knew there were others that were suffering so I started observing it and noticing it in others. For everyone that knew my mother, she was a sweet soul of a woman.

When she had to move into a nursing home because she needed 24 hour attention as her sleeping patterns were off. I was even more heartbroken. It was horrible over those years her body and mind deteriorated faster. All those nursing homes do is drug up their patients and move on. My mom had to be moved a few times and the last time she was hospitalized because no-one had even given my mother water to drink in a week. All her vital organs were close to shut down. Alzheimerz/ dimentia steals the one thing we value most, our minds to operate this world. It is an ugly disease that steals your essence and leaves you to rot in a shell of a your former self. As much as this devastating loss imprisoned me, my mother was the real prisoner, she was locked up inside herself. And knowing that kept me in the deep internal hell.

Baggage is baggage and everybody's got it.

Our relationship within our families as a child matters. How love was expressed or not expressed matters. The family structure matters, lack or loss of family members or the dynamics of how the house functioned matters, the fun and memorable good times or bad times matters. The hurt matters.

We cannot comprehend the suffering many people have gone through. We cannot ever compare our own sorrows. God provides each one of us with the strength it takes to bare the pain of the individual obstacles we face.

We all have the power to bear our own trials.

Some of you have been carrying around the burdens of your painful pasts for a long time. I have great news to share. You can put that baggage down. You have new shit to carry. The bricks of the new creations you are going to be building. It's time to put forth your energy to the New, to the forward, to the now. Your responsibility of doing something meaningful and impactful for you or the world. To make the knowledge and empathy gained from your pains well worth it.

I thought when I hit rock bottom
that would be the foundation I could use
to re-build myself. But then it seemed I hit the magma level.

**What we experience in this life
is spiritual warfare.**

And I learned then that my trials are mandatory
but suffering is a choice.

CHAPTER 13

The Failures

9

The Depression that changes your very being.

I had a small advertising agency at the time of the 2008 financial depression and as you sense this story goes, I lost it. I lost everything. I moved to Florida the summer of 2006 after I purchased my first home the year prior in South Plainfield NJ. I was now living in Coral Springs Florida at the time. As a single mom, I was managing 2 homes in 2 states. I can tell you financially I made a lot of bad decisions with the finances of my company, my ventures, trusting designers or vendors. If I wanted it I would buy it, assuming my business would flourish as I had always imagined it to. I spent money like I shouldn't have. If I needed it, I'd go buy it, without truly being frugal and discerning about it all.

So the reality of losing my home was happening. I had to make a choices: 1. Do I pay my $1800/mo. mortgage in NJ so I don't screw up my credit or do I pay for the $1600 condo payment that was the roof over my sons and my head in Florida. I had to let my home go. I could no longer afford to send the bank my mortgage payment.

By 2008, I was upside down in my home and could not even sell it for what I owed the bank. I was now losing everything. My BMW was about to get repo'd any day. And I just prayed the answers would come. I worked with BMW financial group, making small payments and promising future payments. But I knew it was only a matter of time.

My electric bill was getting paid on the last day before shut off.

Those were some really tough times. I was alone. Possibly facing homelessness and all I did was pray.

It took me a long time to talk about my failures, I was once scarred by them, now I wear them like a tattoo. I have only realized in the past several years that it is critical for us to embrace our failures. This part of me did not define my flaws, it made it obvious to me what was most important to me on how I want to live this life. What I appreciated and what really mattered to me.

Losing Self Worth

Prior to this, I was on a high in my career for many years, making great money, leading great marketing campaigns and making operational business decisions and in an instant it seemed I lost everything. My professional status, my umpf, my mojo. I hit rock bottom emotionally, or at least I thought that was the bottom. Your home and your car define your success in life or at least that's how others see your success. I lost that, I felt like a fool, but I lost something way more valuable than all of those material status symbols combined, I lost my sense of self worth.

How could I ever help others succeed in business if I failed? How can I pick myself up from where I was? I was alone in Florida with my son, no other family and no mother to call or go home to.

I lost my own faith, in my own ability. And I was lost in the trauma of my own mistakes. I blamed myself even though the same things were happening to others all around me. Everybody was suffering financially but I kept replaying the mistakes I made in the early stages of starting my business. I kept replaying in my mind how I could have done things differently. What steps did I fail to take? What else I could have done?

I was a single mom, I was an entrepreneur, I was a risk taker. And I made and took big risks that led to tremendous financial loss.

I felt professionally slaughtered and emotionally broken.

The Dark Room

There is a black room I visit when I want to hide from the rest of the world. Its location is unknown to the public. I go there every time I am emotionally distraught. Every time I think of my mom. Every time I think about the time I was raped, I go in there, every time I think of the time my sense of self worth was challenged. Every time I think about how I could have been a better mother I go in there. Every time I think about mankind's suffering I go in there.

I cry in there, in that dark room. It's an empty room, completely pitch black… but I go in there every time I need to cry. Every time I am overwhelmed with my own being, my own sadness.. Every time I go in I try to find answers for my pain, I try to find logic in the lives of mankind and I beg to be unchained from the sadness I bare.

That room became my refuge, because no one can see or hear me cry in there.

And then I came to realize that my Life had it's own meaning in there. That room gave me justification to fail. It gave me reasons to be lazy. To give up. I was finding it harder and harder to be at peace in there. There was a battle brewing and then it became a war - Between who I know I must become and who I wanted to remain, because I couldn't let go of my sadness.

I stayed in this state of depression for a long time. When my mother finally passed in 2011, I packed a truck and drove my son and I back up to NJ to be back with my sisters.

Mission to Rebuild

I was reading more professional books, more success, more sales books, attending many conferences, high level networking events. I got my fire back. I was feeling my mojo again. Making great money…. But I wasn't wholly happy. I wasn't working for myself and I was choking.

What Actions do you need to take today to get you to where you want to be tomorrow? _____

◆

*"If yesterday was lost in grief,
don't lose today and tomorrow
by keeping your grief in your memory."*

◆

*"Sometimes the bad things that happen in our lives put
us directly on the path to the best things that will ever
happen to us."*

◆

If you pay close enough attention there is something good that comes out of every defeat and every failure. What separates those who are successful from those who are not? The difference between them is the amount of drive and will to go after and pursue ambitions no matter what roadblocks appear. You have the power inside you to pursue and achieve all the goals you can conjure. When you allow roadblocks to stop you, you must admit to yourself you didn't want it bad enough, and then it's your responsibility to find what it is you do want bad enough.

◆

"Anyone who has lost something they thought was theirs forever finally comes to realize that nothing really belongs to them."

-PAULO COELHO

*"You can't have change
and comfort
simultaneously."*

- UNKNOWN

*"When you have exhausted all
possibilities.
Remember this.
You haven't."*

THOMAS A. EDISON

PART 4

MANIFEST DESTINY

CHAPTER 14

Snap Out Of It

9

Rebuilding Self Worth after my Depression

How do you rebuild self worth? By realizing you never lost it.

After the years that followed the 2008 financial collapse, I lost my sense of defining success. And for a little while I lost the courage to really push forward whole heartedly. The things that were once important no longer were, it could have been that I could no longer afford them. But in that I didn't want to talk to anyone. I became distant. I found a new place to hang out, in my solitude.

So I picked up the inner badass within me, gave myself a hard lecture I didn't want to hear.

I am responsible for everything that happens in my life. I must take responsibility for everything that happens in my life. I must make the most of every moment I'm alive and I must be grateful. I must live moving towards my missions. I must move forwards. There are no more pity parties. There is no one coming to rescue me. If I wanted it, I must go get it.

It's time to get to work.

Laziness will paralyze you.

Wallowing in your sorrow will only cause more sorrow.

Create better habits.

Start working within your own structure.

Commit to yourself.

Kick your own ass. <u>No one is going to monitor you</u>. You either are going to do what it takes or your not.

Beating the Self-Limiting Beliefs – You are not good enough. You are not experienced enough. You don't have what it takes. You have so much baggage that if anyone knew about it they would think the worst of you. You shouldn't be happy. You don't measure up. How should you handle this?

Fuck' it. Fuck all of this bullshit. These are all lies. Your mind is using to stay comfortable and not be challenged.

What is fearful is the unknown. We are fearful of not knowing. We are fearful of not having the right answers. We are fearful of making a mistake that may alter our lives or the lives of those we love. We are fearful of looking stupid or bad. Or in a different light of who we know ourselves to be.

But if we create our lives, then suddenly the unknown becomes known.

Fear was created to protect our ancestors, these days it is used to inhibit growth.

Master Fear

If everything is energy, you can learn to master the energy of fear. Most people often feel the energy of fear or anxiety in their throats, in their hearts or in the core chakras. It's the most uncomfortable feeling. Fear can be traumatizing. But it's still energy and energy can transfer, it can move.

Fear of Your Own Voice

How many of you, have emotional overwhelm when you need to speak up at events? Whether it's doing a commercial about your business, or when someone asks you your elevator pitch, or the #1 fear of public speaking. Most of you can relate to this?

When fear comes into your life you need a way to handle it, to manage it, to learn how to overcome it so that it doesn't stop you.

Fear and Excitement Live in the Same Realm of Space

You can learn how to easily convert what your mind perceives as fear into excitement.

Changing fear's name.

Whenever you feel fear come up, change it's name to <u>excitement</u>. When your heart starts to race because you're not sure what to say, change any fear to <u>opportunity</u>.

Embracing the Emotional Overwhelm

Literally, embracing and understanding and accepting that fear shows up in our lives to protect us.

Fear. It sucks And it's going to show up.

Fear can stop you on your journey.

Fear has the ability to control you.

Do Not confuse Fear with Laziness – go ahead and save it for tomorrow, your dreams are so big they can wait another day. Actually, tomorrow might be a better day to get motivated. And another. And another. Why not? Actually stay there in your comfy couch watching Netflix dreaming of your big plans, but never actually doing anything about them.

Agreement Notes:

If you hold Fear responsible for your failures or lack of attempts then you have not fully committed to this life and in possible breach of agreement.

I believe that anyone can conquer fear
by doing the thing he fears to do.

-ELEANOR ROOSEVEL

CHAPTER 15

Self Acceptance

9

First Law of self awareness
It's not them, it's you.

The human mind is a beautiful tool. It can manifest and it can self destruct.

We either often find ourselves fantasizing of the what if's or living in the depressive states of our repetitive pasts.

For some reason our past seams to follow us, and for me the things that hurt me the most are my own fears of my lack in doing the best I could, for my son, my life, my family.

I have given myself the burden of being perfect by this vision I possess in my mind that seems to define perfection. The irony is, that

I don't know anyone who lives that way. It's a vision I have of something I've never seen, and yet I fail to live up to it and I beat myself up for not living up to it. I am in a state of depression." That is how I felt for a long time. Living up to the potential of some imaginary figure of what I designed perfection to look like.

We often allow our pasts to define us. How we grew up and the emotions we've felt growing up, the good memories we've had. They all make us what we are today, right? I thought so for a long time, and because of that, I wasn't letting go. And I was the one being the very block in my life that I needed to get rid of.

We search our whole lives for that thing that will fill the whole in our heart. To be able to feel complete.

Have you ever looked in the mirror to make funny faces just to see what you would look like? If you haven't , you need to put this book down and do it right now. In as much as we are all unique and different, there is an element of similarity between all of us.

We are harshest critics. It's so difficult for us sometimes to come to terms with ourselves, because we know ourselves so well.

Understand Self to Understand Others

Knowing the self – getting to know every egoistic inch of yourself. Only when you can see how selfish you really are, can you begin to free yourself and become a giver.

We are constantly journeying to be developed. We are and all the rest of our days in this life are constantly in a state of progress and work.

God made glorious skies, beautiful oceans, magnificent views, and do you think he loves you less?

And yet we live seeking for the big thrill. We turn to alcohol to dilute the pain of our lives. We turn to drugs to numb our lives.

We are constantly growing, or most of us are anyway. We simply "grow up." Even "gangstas" grow up. Eventually you get to certain stages in life that the childish things you did just aren't important. Your values have changed. You see things from a more mature perspective.

Life is a course – a full-on curriculum. I am an extreme believer in college education. Although I have only a few credits, the concept of learning is one I treasure. I love to learn about things that interest me.

I love the arts, creative, love, spiritual, self-help, psychology and sociology. These are the subjects that interest me... because mankind interests me.

Learning is the part of life that if you put just a bit of dedication towards, you can see remarkable and immeasurable changes in YOU.

See yourself for who you really are

Seek to learn first about you and your own human nature. We can be very observant and judgmental of others- but we often just excuse our own imperfections.

Once you understand you own emotional imbalances, you can start to be sincere to the needs of others.

So how do you start to 'know' yourself? Well first, take a good look in the mirror. And I don't mean look at yourself.. I mean really look at yourself – Look right into your own eyes. And ask yourself –

Do not for one minute think that you are a good, honest and perfect human being. You would be selfish to think that way. You are not and you do need to improve on yourself. Life is a growth process and if you ceased the need to grow, you would not exist.

Emotional self control

Anger is not your normal state. Anger is used to express inner hurt, pain and frustrations. If you come across someone who is angry, show them love and compassion.

◆

Never give anyone or anything the power to
control your emotions.

Never give someone the power to enrage you. Anger is a selfish act. Anger can be a result from being hurt, as if no one is allowed to hurt you. When you expect others to be ignorant and act "stupid" you won't be shocked when they act that way, and you won't have a need to be angry.

You must understand people are going to do stupid things, just as you yourself are capable of doing stupid things.

Support from other

It is often the people we love and care about that can make us angry. Don't put anyone in a position that obligates them to always be "pleasers" in your life. You will always be disappointed. People are bound to screw up just like you are bound to screw up.

Female Emotions

Women are emotional creatures. Everyone should know this by now. And certain times of the month our hormones go astray. Like sometimes I'm like what the heck? Why am I so whiney or emotional, or upset?" Acknowledge this about yourself – 'check yourself' – We can't help the chemistry of our hormones, whether I'm overly sensitive to things or easily agitated during these times. So I often try and pay attention to myself and catch myself if my emotions are overly any one sided. If I find myself snappy or agitated, I quickly remind myself, it's not them, it's me and I'm allowing hormones to get the best of me.

I try and 're-center' myself to my true self. It's important to understand the waves of your emotional states.

Don't be prideful – Don't ever be ashamed or embarrassed to apologize to someone. Whether you find yourself saying something rude or agitated, apologize. Only you have the power to heal and cultivate quality & honest relationships. When you learn to apologize frequently you are acknowledging that you make mistakes, you are human too and you're mature enough to admit your faults and you desire to grow from them. That is growth.

Pride is bad. Apologize when you screw up. Wouldn't it be great if we all did that? And never ever stay angry with someone. Learn to see their side and learn to compromise. Relationships in life are give and take, if you want your point to be accepted, learn to accept others and if you care enough about someone try to see where they are coming from.

Be compassionate, be kind.

The thing about compassion and kindness is that it is almost always reciprocated.

Keep reminding yourself that the same inner and personal struggles and emotions you face, so does your neighbor, friend and stranger.

The saddest thing about mankind is the lack of compassion and understanding for one another. We all have the same problems. We all experience the same things. We all share the same types of emotions; yet it is hard for us to put ourselves in the shoes of another and feel a sense of humility and compassion and understanding for what that another person is going through.

Everyone wants to feel like no one could possibly understand their life. But it's all relative.

◆

See yourself in others,
see others as family members of those you love
and those you hold most dear.
And you can easily start to see them as love
and relate to them as part of you and not a stranger.

All of the significant battles
are waged within the self.

- SHELDON KOPP

Living with intention is saying "fuck it, whatever happens, I'm going for it. I'm going to live this life and follow it's trail wherever it may lead, I'm open to all that the universe has in store for me. I'm open to my responsibility to create a life that is meaningful to me.

CHAPTER 16

Pillar Of Energy

9

Everything is energy, that's all there is to it. Match the frequency of the reality you want and you cannot help but get that reality. It can be no other way. This is not philosophy. This is physics.

ALBERT EINSTEIN

You are energy. You operate on a frequency that is constantly sending and receiving signals from everything around us. What signals are you sending? What signals are you picking up on?

Mastering you energy is probably the most critical pillar of this life. Your energy is your life. Everything you are is controlled at this level. If you want to change anything about your life, you start with energy.

Things that affect your energy.

Everything.

Internal Emotions. External Circumstances.

Monkey minds & fake stories

Health & Wellbeing

"Everything we see, hear and feel can be measured by vibrational energy. Yet, less than 1% have any idea how to blueprint their energy to accelerate their abilities to access success and mastery with their bodies."

Take a moment to breathe here.

Put everything down and take a few deep breaths. Sit there feel your body. When you take your next breath, imagine you inhaling the energy of God. Because you are, you need that breath to exist. And that breath is God.

Keep that in mind. Don't take your breaths for granted. Every moment matters. Every breath matters. And with every breath remember the God is within you.

There is majestic Life force energy that is dancing through your body right now. It's God. And it's You. Do you feel the essence of your complexity? It's a beautiful science built on perfect love. And it resides within you, guiding you, supporting you.

Controlling Monkey Minds

It's time to take full responsibility over the powers you have been given and how you are using it.

Controlling your energy begins in the mind. Our minds are constantly flooded with thoughts, memories and consistent external stimulation.

Monkey minds are when our minds go on a rampage, going through so many various thoughts that it almost immobilizes you. You don't know what to work on next, you don't know if you have the confidence to do that thing.

******

But you can **choose the thoughts** you have. Whether you are choosing to be happy or think good thoughts you will be happy and fun to be around for others.

When you think negative thoughts, when you think about the "what if's ", when you assume you know the intention of other people, you will find yourself feeling negative. Your negative energy will have an influence on the vibes you give off. And you will not be fun to be around.

Master Your Energy

Science tells us that at our core we are vibrational energy. Literal vibrating atoms that are not even a solid.

Many eastern practices are based on understanding the energy life force and how to tap and use it to our advantage. How to flow with it, how to dance with it and how to manipulate it. For healings, for medicinal practices, for soulful connections and to co-create our lives.

➤ Meditation

➤ Body Health

➤ Energy Tapping

➤ Neural Conditioning

It's important you seek out deeper understandings of these practices as they give you deeper insights about your own spirituality. You cannot ignore the spirituality and love within these energetic motions.

We are a force.

We are moving and vibrating with every absolute thing around us.

1. The Ability of Your Energy

Our energy has the ability to attract or deter situations and people in our lives.

How we think about someone and mostly how we think about our selves in front of that someone. This can give off the corresponding energy to let that person know how you feel without saying a single word. You are thinking negative thoughts, you start feeling yucky inside and you emote this energy letting others know something is bothering you.

You can change this.

2. Relational Energy

You can change the vibe of a room by what you bring to it. And you are totally responsible for the energy you contribute to the world. Because knowing that you have this power, gives you the responsibility to use it for good.

You are responsible for how you wish to use your Energy powers. If you want love and positive things around you, give love and positivity to the world. If you want kindness, give kindness. Give to others what you hope or expect them to give to you. What you exude in your essence, you will get back in essence.

3. Internal Emotions

First step is to be self aware that the thoughts in your head impact your emotions and your energy. If you are feeling insecure or are thinking that someone is judging you, and your fighting with that person, in your head with that person.. start looking for something you do like about that person. To be honest people are more worried about the drama and others in their own lives than they are about you. Don't let your ego control you.

Start thinking about a good loving thought. Something funny your kids did, something loving your spouse did, something kind a friend did. Capture your negative thoughts, change your script and you will stop worrying about negative shit that doesn't matter and you will remember to live in the moment. You will exude positive good vibrations and others will treat you better.

You can impact all of these factors in your life by the types of thoughts you decide to keep.

Are you finding yourself judging people who you simply "sense" are judging you?

You have everything you need.

You are life force energy. You have at your disposal all the tools and gifts of the gods. You have everything to create, design and manifest any life you desire to. When you take ownership of your toolbox, you start learning how to sharpen these tools in your life so you can create your best work.

There are leaders and prophets, philosophers and Einstein's, and many before you that have paved roads for us.

Whether you enjoy reading & seeking truths, or you already sense it inside you. The energy and ability you have inside you can help you become any thing and any one and achieve any dream you desire. For every desire there is an execution plan. Create an execution plan.

Trust yourself, Make a plan, Take action.

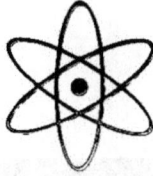

Everything is energy,

that's all there is to it.

Match the frequency of

the reality you want

and you cannot help

but get that reality.

It can be no other way.

This is not philosophy.

This is physics.

ALBERT EINSTEIN

Maybe it was there all along...and it takes the darkness
to reveal the beauty.

CHAPTER 17

Where Change Begins

9

How often are you doing things that grow you? How often are you learning something new or refining your skills.

You must commit to your own evolution & self-growth – if you don't, you will miss the bigger picture.

1. Be the Sponge

Be a student, a sponge, consume goodness. I used to always say 'Chew the meat and spit out the bones' – but as a Plant Based foodie these days, it no longer sounds right to me. But what I'm referring to is consume all love and loving messages and speaks love to your heart.

2. Look for the goodness in all life.

Part of Self Growth is understanding and accepting all that is. It is an awareness of the beauty of life. An appreciation and gratitude for every thing. This includes everything you do and do not understand.

Be open to seeing goodness by looking for a lesson that allows your intellect or heart to grow. How does that experience make you feel? Look for love in your experiences. And often you will find it. If we look for troubles we will find them. Always seek out the light in others. Be the example to others of how you want them to be with you. You will find it.

3. Look for Lessons

There are 4 Areas of Life Success.

Mind, Body, Soul, Business

View alternate perspectives and global understandings.

Be willing to test and question what you think you know.

Your light is continual evolving higher consciousness

Commit to Evolve for the better in all aspects of your life.

You are responsible for your life, even all that you feel is not right within it.

No one is obligated to appease to your good senses. The only person responsible for your life is you. The evolution of understanding that with your mind you have the gift and the true energetic power to create a hell out of heaven and a heaven out of hell.

You are committed to doing what it takes.

To be in a state of self growth, it means there are days or weeks that you don't really sleep, but there are also days and weeks where you don't work. It's about finding a balance that works for the comfort of your own life. Finding what makes you happy. What fulfills you. And do not be afraid to have a bunch of different things. My boyfriend has often called me a contradiction. I think it's part of my beauty as a women. My ability to see all sides and accept the sides that which I don't see. Life is a myriad of beautiful uncertainties, but it is also a beautiful myriad of many truths. We are guided by a source of love and we have the ability to move our energy.

Without knowledge,
your goals become elusive.

For this is the journey that men make: to find themselves. If they fail in this, it doesn't matter much what else they find.

– JAMES A. MICHENER

CHAPTER 18

Pillar Of Fuck-Its

9

So you fucked up?

Who gives a fuck?

It's time to realize all the bullshit fake shit.

This life is spiritual

Much more tangible than the material

Fuck" all the fake shit that stresses you out.

If it ain't coming from a place of love, Fuck It.

If they judge you, Fuck it.

If you fuck up, fuck it.

Do You. Live You.

Go for it, Fuck it.

And create a Fucking amazing life.

Because otherwise you'll be fucked.

Look for the critics, look for the judgments, if you are being criticized, it's because you have decided to do something. You are not sitting on your ass as a spectator. You are doing what others wish they had the courage to do. Yes it can be uncomfortable, but what's worse is being the one sitting on their couch watching others pursue something while you only wished you could.

Have a Fuck it mentality, because really, fuck it! What do you have to lose? You're going to die one day.

Fuck what other people think, sometimes even your own self judgment.

1)   You can't allow the judgment of others stop you from doing and becoming all that you desire to do and become in this life.

2)   And Fuck your own self doubts.

People are gonna judge you – "fuck'm and stop thinking about it.

The irony – You are probably judging them more for judging you. Pay attention to the adjectives and emotions you feel about a person You are not going to stop them. So why focus brain cells on worry and stress about what they think of you, when you can stay focused on your own success.

So don't give a fuck about anyone else passing judgment on you. You are doing your thing, your purpose. Don't let anyone stop you. You'll die with regrets.

And Fuck that.

People are not as concerned about you as you think they are. They are not constantly thinking about you and your fuck up. They are thinking about their own lives. And if they are, you won't ever know, and it doesn't even matter.

You need to stay focused on your own life and what you want to do and what you need to do and doing those things. Stop worrying about what others think and worry about what you think of yourself if you don't ever get to live out your dreams.

Fuck your own self judgment

Fuck the judgment, fuck the self-doubt, fuck the fear. Go all in. Because one day you look and it's today. And you think to yourself, you should have been farther along in life already. You were expecting to be. You didn't get to accomplish all the things you thought you would have already achieved. You shame yourself and you feel behind everyone else. The good news is, that thought is bullshit. And you have This Life, right here and right now.

CHAPTER 19

Forgiveness

9

Forgiveness liberates the soul. It removes fear. That is why it is such a powerful weapon. Nelson Mandela

You have a lot to forgive yourself about. Not that you've done a lot of bad or shitty things. But you think you did. So you're holding on to it. And it's time to let it go.

Self Forgiveness

In life we want a lot of things, forgiveness is something we need. We need other people to forgive us but we need to forgive ourselves.

All the things you're holding onto, all of those mistakes, regrets, what if's, should have's and could have's. You are giving them way too much energy.

Forgive yourself for not speaking up.
Forgive yourself for speaking up.
We need to forgive ourselves
Find out what it is you are holding onto. Find what it is that is a burdon on your back and forgive yourself. Show empathy and compassion for yourself.

You are no longer your past, in fact you can actually change your past. To begin, you must forgive yourself for all that baggage of remorse, regret and pain you've been carrying around, hiding behind a smile.

It's time to Forgive Yourself.
Now Forgive others.

Forgive Family,

Forgive Friends,
Forgive Enemies,
Forgive your baby daddy
Forgive you neighbor
Forgive someone who has stolen from you
Forgive anyone who has hurt you
And all those whome you are cautious that will.

Forgive Everyone

We are passionate and emotional beings and because of that, we tend to beat ourselves up over some of the most mundane of things. Forgive yourself for everything you thought you should have, could have done. Forgive and move forward. Your time is now. Your moment to erase the past is now. Do everything you thought you should have done then, right now. So you don't look back and regret what you could have done today. Your moment is now!

To understand everything is to forgive everything.

– BUDDHA.

No one is obligated to you.

Being independent & self-reliant is a self-responsibility. Every thing you need to drive your life is inside you. And you can access your god-ness abilities at any time.

Be patient
toward all that is unresolved in your heart
and try to love the questions themselves.

- Rainer Maria Rilke

We all have a story.

We have all suffered.

Now What?

◆

The person you want to become requires effort. It is under the deepest of pressure that you are transformed into your magnificence. You have to be ready to step outside your comfort zone. The person you want to be is going to require you to get uncomfortable. It's going to require a new version of you. One whose bravery is growing daily. Keep going.

Your problem isn't ideas

or lack of knowledge,

your problem is

you're not taking the action to manifest them.

CHAPTER 20

Fluid Motion

9

Be like water

Flow with life's tide and ride the wave.

What are the stories you need to come face to face and mourn ?

What are the beliefs about you and those stories?

What emotions do you feel?

When you visit www.TheLifeAgreement.com you can request special time with me should you want to address this on a much deeper 1 on 1 level but for now let's get to it.

Because You are Amazing.

Let me share with you how fucking amazing you are, so you can stop looking for flaws and you can begin to celebrate your perfect genius so you can flow with life instead of fighting it.

You must never be afraid to be who you are or think as you do. You are made of love child, be love. It's your genius. Too much of a conditioned society has made us feel insecure in our thought process and in our inner passions. But also flow with the need to evolve to your capabilities.

Accept your crazy thoughts, but be willing to challenge them.

"Be **like water** making its way through cracks. Do not be assertive, but adjust to the object, and you shall find a way around or through it. If nothing within you stays rigid, outward things will disclose themselves. Empty your mind, be formless. Shapeless, **like water**. If you put **water** into a cup, it becomes the cup. You put water into a bottle and it becomes the bottle. You put it in a teapot, it becomes the teapot. Now, water can flow or it can crash. Be water, my friend."

-                                   Bruce   Lee

CHAPTER 21

Intentions

9

Your evolution is an expression of gratitude towards the Universe. Your willingness to evolve is an expression of self-love.

Everything you decide to do and feel going forward from this moment is in your hands.

What do you Intend to do?

This life that you were given comes with one shot, one opportunity. You have an obligation to yourself to use this life to its fullest; you have a responsibility to become all that you wish to become; and you have been missioned to create the life you want to live and you are gifted with the ability to make it all happen.

So why aren't more people living this life as if they own it?

Many have this big picture of their passions. Sometimes your heart speaks a language than can be difficult to interpret and you find it difficult to express in words. If you have a calling to help others, if you have a calling to empower others, you have to have the daily intention and daily habits that will support the life you are intending to live.

Sometimes life gets so busy managing the family, kids, school, work, career, your true heart's mission, vision or joy gets put on the back burner.

> *"Whether you think you can or can't,*
> *you're probably right."*

Boulder Ready

Boulder's are going to be there. It's your ability to understand that and learn the tools you will need to move past them.

Going after your dreams, takes bravery, it takes devotion & effort, it takes action and it takes the willingness to be seen and judged and saying "Fuck it, I'd rather go for it and fail, then not go for it and regret."

Everyone is going to judge you. Everyone is going to have an opinion. Your family may not support you or really care about your aspirations.

People are not only scared to go after their dreams,

People are scared to dream simply because they fear what others will negatively think of them. Some of the boulders we will face are the self-doubting thoughts make their way into the forefront of our thoughts.

Some want to live the same routine life every day and choose not to do anything to ambitious with their life. That may work for them, but it shouldn't work for you. You have a purpose here. You have a mission, something you need to do, something that matters

What new face courage puts on everything.

– RALPH WALDO EMERSON

What are the risks of not going all in?

A life you are not content with. A purpose left unfulfilled.

Some of the biggest regrets you will hear about, is the regret of not having the audacity to pursue dreams and overcome fears.

People regret the chances they didn't take. Heck, you probably regret something about yesterday or 10 years ago or 30 years ago.

For many years I struggled with sharing my story. I didn't know where to start. I didn't know what was important. I didn't want to come off any particular way. I feared judgment. I feared what others would think of me. But mostly, every time I began to put words to paper. I wrote freely... I cried freely.. It was therapy for myself.

But today, I am Free.

This book is not an autobiography so I will try and give you a visual of the framework I was working with.

In 1999 exactly 8 months after my brother was found dead from a Heroin overdose, we found out my mother, at 53 years old, was diagnosed with advanced alzheimers. I held on to a lot of emotions for a long time about this.

This regret did 2 things: It put me in longsuffering mourning. It made me sad and that sadness scared me and in so many ways.

And second, it empowered me. It taught me to " Fuck it do it," because I realized I was certain life was too short to not live fully.

Time...

Enjoying every moment is critical. Don't wait for tomorrow to be happy. Don't wait to win the lottery, don't wait till you get a better job, don't wait till you have more courage. Every moment matters.

So what do you want to accomplish & how do you want to feel?

_____

This can be answered by grabbing a pen and paper and begin asking yourself these questions.

- Who do you wish to become?

- What do you wish to see in the world?

- What makes you happy?

This Life Agreement is here to support you in becoming who it is you want to become, so that you can take all the chances you desire to take, to live your life with bliss and no regrets.

- You are buying this life. You are buying this body, this time, these years.

- Now it's time to do something great with it.

- You have 1 life, 1 shot, 1 chance... and the time to do something about it is right now.

- Nothing that has happened to you in the past matters.

- Your upbringing doesn't matter.

- What you had or didn't have, it doesn't matter.

- All the worry in the world will not solve your sorrows.

- All the complaining won't manifest joy.

- Don't find yourself holding on to unnecessary baggage.

- Don't find yourself with regrets.

Learn to live your life so fully that your days are filled with joy at gratitude for the simplest.

The person you want to become requires effort. It is under the deepest of pressure that you are transformed into your magnificence. You have to be ready & willing to step outside your comfort zone. You have to understand that the person you want to be is just over that peak. Keep climbing.

This Life Agreement will help you rekindle your own fire, kick your own ass and shine.

No amount of worry about the future, no amount of sadness about the past has the ability to stop a determined mind.

If death is certain and it's going to come fast, why not live, every day like you exist for a greater purpose?

Go pursue with the mission of being happy to be alive and do something that makes a difference and contributes goodness for others.

There is a child inside of you that once believed and sometimes remembers that everything is possible. At some point that child stopped believing in the magic of life's possibilities. Find that again.

Fly. Somewhere.

Everybody has dreams.
It's about who is going out and
doing something about it.

CHAPTER 22

Poetry And Prose

In the midst of all that I am
I am free to be
I have been given a gift
A gift of reason
A gift of desire for wisdom
A gift of purpose
And meaning
And life

In the midst of all that I am
The collection of my desires
Of all my dreams
The whole of my existence
Is measured by my mere efforts
To manifest my thoughts
In the midst of all that I am,
I am a Creator

◆

By all reason, and in many forms
Lies the power we possess within us
To do all that is challenged around us
It is the same power, the same force
That birthed my desire for servitude.

◆

On the journey to joy
Trials bring strength,
Sorrow is a teacher

◆

You are what you consume
That which you allow into your mind
Only a figment be destroyed by the wind
What does your heart desire?

What goes in is what comes out
Absorb goodness and give it
Why is it so hard to love
a stranger and any common man?

Hurt by our transgressions
Hatred becomes the broken man
Deep beyond his wounds his memory reflects
There is hurt and pain in all of us.

All that I am and all that I wish to become
Is but a moment in time
I have consumed the very essence that I desire to be
To be the gift that God has given me
My spirit, my purpose, my life.

◆

I am merely a product of my own creation.

A figment of my imagination

Everything that I aspire to be

A noted creation of my thoughts

I am what I believe in my heart

In the midst of it all

Life's ups and life's downs

I am joyful that I know

We are One.

◆

I have been captured

I am held hostage

I am a prisoner

To my own demise

I have been searching

I have yet no answer

I am burning in anguish

Deep inside

I cause my paths

Both good and bad

I am to learn

I must obey

The pain I feel

This giant wound

May never go away

◆

In my pain and burdens
I am compelled to reach higher
In my turmoil
I find the peace within.
In my sadness
I am covered by the grace of a loving Universe.

◆

I Promise to:
Think
Inspire
Contribute
Serve

Humanity.

Interesting to some

Boring to others

Beautiful to many

Ugly to most

I am a book

Except my pages are being created as you progress through

I have a beautiful ending

I have a complicated journey

It's different for every set of eyes

I am a mystery, a journal, a biography

A novel intended to expand perspective

I am full of mistakes, I need major editing

I desire to be polished so that I can make it in the hands of love

But then I realized I am love.

I am a book

◆

Human Life is about a journey of progression and fulfillment
An ever-changing journey of experiences.
Life is Growth.
Life is about Experiences, Lessons & Change
Inevitable Soul Development
Understanding & Compassion
Statue of Worthiness
Army Readiness
Manifest Change
The Power of God

◆

How can I express to you
How I feel
I can only feel
This pain
This torment
These mistakes
Trapped in my today
Grains of yesterday
I'm ready for tomorrow
Yet I can't let go

◆

No amount of worry about the future,
no amount of sadness about the past
has the ability to stop
a determined mind

◆

.

CHAPTER 24

The Life Agreement

9

THIS AGREEMENT (the "Agreement") dated this _____
day of _____(month), _____ (year)

The Source of All Life

- AND -

(YOU) _____

3) I, the undersigned, commit and agree to furnish all action and labor to design and create the **life of my dreams**.

4) I hereby commit to doing whatever it takes, to nurture my own health and wellbeing. To ensure I address areas of my life that may hold me back.

5) I commit to be honest with myself.

6) I commit to being honest with others.

7) I understand fully that not taking action may result in misery.

8) I understand that not taking care of my mind's health and my body's wellbeing I will suffer beyond reason.

9) I will achieve the greatness that I know is within me.

10) I will pay the price that is necessary to reach my life's purpose Because I know that not fulfilling my purpose will leave me feeling short-changed in my life.

11) I understand fully that the life I design will be reached one action step at a time, with each step bringing me closer to the **life of my dreams**.

12) I will not settle for living a life less than ideal for myself.

13) I understand the life I want to lead is ready and willing to manifest itself so long as I pursue it with action.

14) I have the passion, the power, the will and the knowledge to create life on my terms.

15) I understand that the Universe is ready to support me in everything I do and so long as I pursue the knowledge I need, it will show up for me.

16) I understand I must be the one to Pursue My Dreams

17) I commit to Living the live of my dreams.

18) Time is of the Essence

IN CONSIDERATION OF the matters described above and of the mutual benefits and obligations set forth.

Repeat: Time is of the Essence.

Your Signature

Signature of Your Commitment

Thank You!

Please Connect With Me on Social Media.

SandraNoemi.com

To receive private coaching in support of your success please contact me or visit my website at **SandraNoemi.com** to schedule a consultation.

www.ingramcontent.com/pod-product-compliance
Lightning Source LLC
Chambersburg PA
CBHW070036100426
42740CB00013B/2709

9 780692 130704